PABLO PICASSO

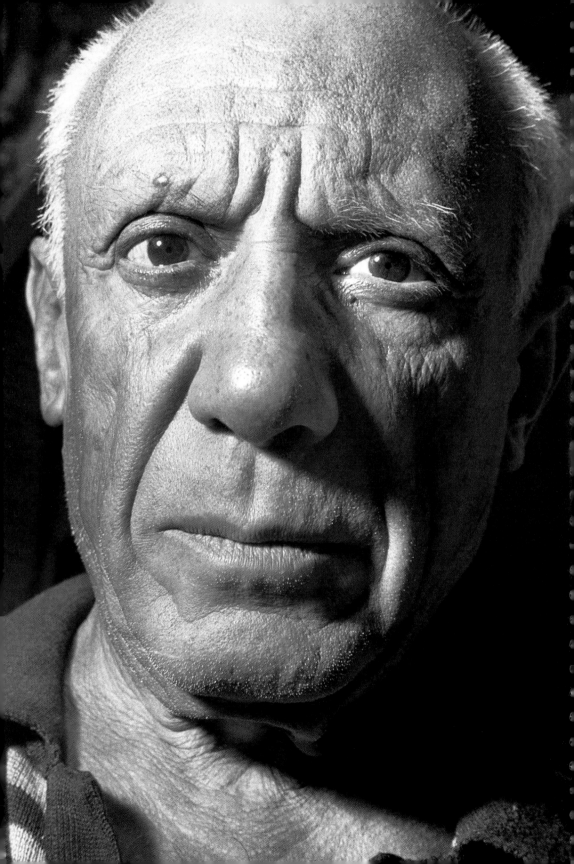

PABLO PICASSO

JENNIFER FANDEL

CREATIVE EDUCATION · CREATIVE PAPERBACKS

Published by Creative Education and Creative Paperbacks
P.O. Box 227, Mankato, Minnesota 56002
Creative Education and Creative Paperbacks are imprints of
The Creative Company
www.thecreativecompany.us

Book design by Blue Design (www.bluedes.com)
Art direction by Rita Marshall
Printed in China

Photographs by Art Resource, NY (Réunion des Musées Nationaux), Corbis
(Archivo Iconografico, S.A., Bettmann, Alexander Burkatovski, Burstein
Collection, Christie's Images, Condé Nast Archive, Edimédia, Hulton-Deutsch
Collection, Francis G. Mayer, Gail Mooney, Philadelphia Museum of Art, Photo
Collection Alexander Alland Sr.), Museu Picasso, Barcelona © 2004 Estate of
Pablo Picasso/Artist Rights Society (ARS), New York

Excerpts on pp. 56–66 and pp. 66–73 from *Artists on Art*, compiled and edited
by Robert Goldwater and Marco Treves. © 1945 by Pantheon Books and
renewed 1973 by Robert Goldwater and Marco Treves. Used by permission of
Pantheon Books, a division of Random House, Inc.

Library of Congress Cataloging-in-Publication Data
Fandel, Jennifer.
Pablo Picasso / Jennifer Fandel.
p. cm. — (Odysseys in artistry)
Includes bibliographical references and index.
Summary: A biography of Spanish-born artist Pablo Picasso, examining his
development of the Cubist style and his social commentary, as well as many of
his greatest paintings.

ISBN 978-1-60818-720-1 (hardcover)
ISBN 978-1-62832-316-0 (pbk)
ISBN 978-1-56660-786-5 (eBook)
1. Picasso, Pablo, 1881–1973—Juvenile literature. 2. Artists—France—Biography—
Juvenile literature.

N6853.P5 F36 2016
709.2—dc23   2015048540

CCSS; RI.8.1, 2, 3, 4; RI.9-10.1, 2, 3, 4; RI.11-12.1, 2, 3, 4; RH.6-8.1, 4, 5, 7;
RH.9-10.1, 3, 4

First Edition HC 9 8 7 6 5 4 3 2 1
First Edition PBK 9 8 7 6 5 4 3 2 1

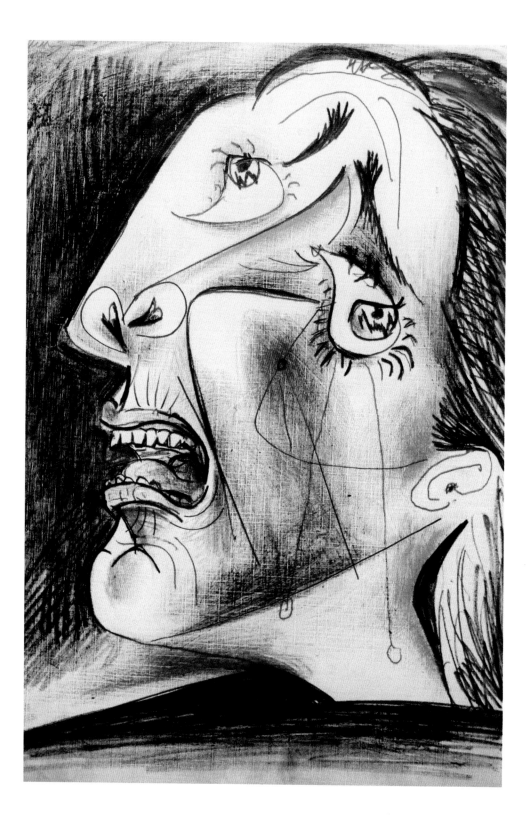

CONTENTS

The Birth of a Genius

Pablo's mother saw the spark of genius early in her son's dark, curious eyes. Throughout his childhood, she loved to say, "If you become a soldier, you'll be a general. If you become a monk, you'll end up Pope!" Whenever he recalled his mother's words as an adult, Pablo always smiled, adding, "Instead I became a painter and ended up Picasso!" One of the

OPPOSITE: The theme of a mother and child was one that Picasso revisited in various stages of his artistic career, thanks in part, perhaps, to his own relationship with his mother.

most prolific and idolized artists of the 20th century, Pablo Picasso continually broke artistic boundaries and stunned the world with his originality. Decades after the artist's death, his name still resonates with boldness, and his work reveals the vision of a man driven to create until the very end.

Pablo Ruiz Picasso was born on October 25, 1881, in Málaga, a town in the sun-drenched south of Spain. His father, José Ruiz Blasco, was a painter who had struggled for years to make a living as an artist. Shortly after his marriage to Maria Picasso, José accepted that he would never become a great artist and settled into a job teaching art. As a teacher, he was able to provide a comfortable, middle-class lifestyle for his wife and family, but he often felt dissatisfied. He hoped that Pablo, his only son, would have the opportunity to achieve greater success in his life than he had in his own.

Pablo, the eldest of the Ruiz children, had two sisters. His sister Lola was born on the heels of an earthquake, a terrifying experience for three-year-old Pablo. Already an imaginative boy, he could not look at his sister without conjuring visions of the earthquake. He regarded the shift of the earth as the moment when his parents' attention shifted away from him to the new baby. Pablo's other sister, Conchita, born when Pablo was six, died as a child. The loss was difficult for the whole family, but it was especially hard on Pablo's father, plunging him into a lasting depression.

Pablo took after his mother physically, with large, dark eyes and black hair that swept across his forehead, but he seemed to possess equal amounts of his parents' personalities. He had his mother's fun-loving spirit and was often full of mischief, his eyes flashing and his mouth bent into a smirk. But, like his father, he was also moody. Pablo's face could cloud over with seriousness in an instant.

As a toddler, shapes and colors enchanted Pablo, and the first word he uttered was "*piz*," short for *lápiz*, or "pencil." From the moment his parents placed a pencil in his hand, Pablo began to understand the correlation between pictures and the expression of ideas and emotions. Drawing spirals was his way of telling his parents that he wanted a *churro*, a sweet Spanish pastry. Shapes and colors, Pablo learned, could bring the world to his feet.

T hroughout his childhood, Pablo spent long hours each day drawing everything that came before his eyes. His parents could see that he had talent, but they worried over Pablo's difficulties and disinterest in school. Day after day, Pablo's attention drifted away from his lessons to the imaginary world he created with his pen. In elementary school, reading, writing, and arithmetic remained troublesome for him, a sign that he perhaps had

a learning disability. Simple addition was a mystery. The only way he seemed to understand the numbers were as shapes: the zero like the eye of a pigeon, the two like the shape of its wing.

While he always made friends easily, Pablo often preferred the companionship of his paper and pen. Given the influence of his artistic father, Pablo's leanings toward art seemed quite natural. He often listened when artists stopped by to discuss their work, and he followed the examples of his father's paintings that hung throughout the family home. From an early age, Pablo shared his father's artistic passion for pigeons and bullfights. He studied his father's model pigeons, trying to capture their shape and texture. And, after an afternoon at the bullfights with his father, Pablo spent hours sketching the motion of the bull and matador in their dance with death.

Dia 8 de Octubre de 1893

10 cs

Azul y Blanco

N.º 1

Se publica todos los domingos

Telegramas

Madrid

A la hora de entrar en maquina este periódico no se recibió ningun telegrama.

"He collected musical instrument cases and old, chipped, ugly frames. Pale prints, with frames made of straw, hung on the dining-room wall…. He prided himself on seeing charm in things which would have seemed ridiculous to most people."

— Fernande Olivier, Picasso's companion in Paris

Under his father's watchful eye and constant encouragement, Pablo perfected his drawing skills, but as he grew older, he saw differences between his father's art and his own. His father, who followed all of the academic rules of painting, created docile still lifes and landscapes to decorate people's homes. Knowing that he wanted to do more with his talent, the teenager broke away from his father's rigid ideas about art and relied on his own creative impulses. When José realized that his 14-year-old son had already reached his own level of artistic skill, he handed over his paints and brushes, symbolically stepping aside to let Pablo's genius flourish.

His Dark, Determined Stare

In 1895, Pablo's family moved to Barcelona, a vibrant city along the northern Mediterranean coast, near France. In his first formal step away from his father's artistic guidance, Pablo enrolled at Barcelona's La Lonja School of Fine Arts. Given a month to complete his entrance exam, he took only one day, rendering the nude model with perfection. At La Lonja, Pablo attended classes with young men five and six years older than

OPPOSITE: The sharp intensity of his eyes was a defining characteristic of Picasso throughout his life and conveyed his fierce independence.

himself, yet his talents surpassed those of his skilled classmates. He found art classes boring and ridiculed the "establishment art" he felt they were being taught to produce. Pablo's father and teacher quickly realized that Pablo was beyond the training provided at La Lonja, but they were reluctant to set the teenager free, without any supervision or structure.

At the age of 15, without prompting or encouragement, Pablo painted three large compositions for competition. One of the paintings was selected for inclusion in the Barcelona city show, an exhibition of Barcelona's best painters, and another received an honorable mention at the Madrid General Fine Arts Exposition. At last, afraid of hampering his son's development, José sent Pablo to school in the fast-paced capital city of Madrid when he turned 16. There Pablo found the same rigid rules about the creation of art, but, away from his father's gaze, he skipped school and studied on his own, absorbing life on the Madrid streets and spending long hours at The Prado, the national art museum. His favorite canvases were by renowned Spanish painters such as El Greco and Diego Velázquez, who painted in the 16th and 17th centuries, and Francisco de Goya, who painted in the late 1700s and early 1800s. Standing before each of the paintings, Pablo looked beyond the artists' obvious talents and studied how their brushstrokes,

colors, and compositions rendered their particular visions of the world.

Returning home after a few months in Madrid, Pablo traveled with a close friend from school to a small farming village in the mountains. While visiting the friend's family there, Pablo befriended a young **gypsy** and became enamored of the simple life he lived. Inspired by the gypsy's freedom, Pablo refused to return to school and moved out of his parents' house. Before his 18th birthday, he struck out on his own as an artist, although he still relied on financial support from his family and friends.

Pablo worked long hours in his Barcelona studio, but he loved to join other aspiring artists and writers for nightly camaraderie at a cafe called *Els Quatre Gats* (The Four Cats). Pablo lingered at the cafe late into the night, listening as the others gave speeches, read poems, argued, and shared their ideas and visions. Pablo was captivated by the bohemian lifestyle of his fellow artists, driven to create and live free from the monotony and constraints of ordinary life. Whenever Pablo's father saw him, dressed in his ragged, paint-splattered clothes, with a beret dipped over his eye, José worried that his son was becoming a bum. The emotional distance between them widened, and Pablo's stubborn resistance to his father's ideals showed in his dark, determined stare.

Pablo's nightly visits to The Four Cats were part of a larger movement in art throughout Europe in the late 1800s. Young artists, looking toward the coming century as a time of great change, rebelled against previous movements in art and pursued their own new visions. The Modernist movement—dynamic, experimental, and often startling—took its foothold in the vibrant city of

Paris, drawing artists from around the world. In 1900, Pablo, too, packed a bag and boarded a train to France.

The young artist was overcome by what he saw in Paris: couples kissing on street corners and park benches; endless rows of dance halls, cafes, and cabarets; and a wild assortment of vendors, artists, vagrants, and painted prostitutes lingering on the streets. Bright, daring, alive with music, and brimming with conversation, Paris was grander than Pablo had imagined. He visited the city frequently over the next few years to stimulate his creativity. Regardless of the season or time of day, Paris pulsed with artistic energy and ideas, encouraging Pablo's venture into boldness.

Into the Spotlight

In 1904, at the age of 22, Pablo moved
to Paris permanently, settling in a run-
down area where many struggling
artists lived. His apartment, doubling
as a studio, had thin walls, creaking
floors, and no running water. Tubes of
paint littered the floor, canvases were
strewn across his bed and propped
inside the bathtub, and cobwebs
graced high corners of the room.
Pablo, who could not afford to eat
every day, refused to "sell out" and get

OPPOSITE: Café de la Rotonde is a famous bohemian cafe in the
Montparnasse Quarter of Paris.

a regular job to support himself, relying instead on the help of friends when his paintings didn't sell. When he wrote to his family, he tried to disguise his hardships, boasting of his small successes. He would not visit home until he could impress his family with a steady income from painting.

Around this time, Pablo began using his mother's name, Picasso, when he signed his work. His father's name, Ruiz, was heard often in Spain, but "Picasso" was uncommon, original, and memorable. Pablo went to art shows and cafes, immersing himself in the art world and making friends with an ever-growing circle of artists, writers, and intellectuals. At the age of 23, Pablo met Fernande Olivier, who remained his constant companion for more than seven years. However, there was little separation between Pablo's personal life and his art. Like many other women in Pablo's future, Fernande became his model and his muse, and the canvas revealed Pablo's deepest emotions, both loving and harsh, toward her.

In his early 20s, Pablo experimented with many different ideas and styles in his art. Because of his obsessive use of blue and rose hues, his early paintings became classified as **Blue Period** and **Rose Period** works. While Pablo often claimed that his ideas sprang only from his imagination, his study of art contributed greatly to his paintings. In 1906, he developed a fascination with African and **pre-Iberian art**, studying masks and figures of the human form. The angular, distorted faces and bodies intrigued Pablo and fellow artist Georges Braque. Copying many of the shapes into their own paintings, Pablo and Braque looked for the shapes, light, and angles that made up an object. They also experimented with perspective by presenting multiple sides of an object at once. This led to the art movement called **Cubism**.

In the spring of 1907, Pablo unveiled *Les Demoiselles d'Avignon*, his first painting in the Cubist style. Artists, friends, and art dealers were stunned, and many thought that Pablo had lost his mind. The portrayal of the women seemed primitive, almost as if they wore masks, and Pablo's new use of perspective perplexed viewers. Nevertheless, art dealer Daniel-Henry Kahnweiler saw brilliance in the new work. His instinct told him that Pablo's paintings would soon be recognized in the art world. He had faith that time would change people's minds.

In 1913, Kahnweiler's predictions came true: Cubism soared in popularity. At a major art auction, with the work of both new and well-established artists on

the block, Pablo's work commanded the highest prices, making him, in only one day, both rich and famous in the art world. At only 32 years old, Pablo and the "Picasso" name were known internationally.

Unfortunately, with his newfound success, Pablo grew increasingly self-centered about his career, viewing his relationships with friends and lovers as stepping-stones or obstacles to his future successes. When many of his French friends left Paris to fight in World War I, Pablo thought of them and the war very little, except to lament the disintegration of their artistic community. In 1918, he married Olga Koklova, a Russian ballerina with ties to royalty and high society, hoping her wealth and connections would influence his career. Following the birth of their son, Paul, Pablo took a mistress, Marie-Thérèse Walter, with whom he had another child, a girl named

Maya. He eventually separated from Olga in 1935, but Marie-Thérèse would remain his mistress for the next two decades.

As life grew progressively tumultuous for him, Pablo poured himself into his work. No matter whose heart he had broken, no matter who wanted more of his time or attention, no matter which friends had died on the battlefront or returned home wounded, Pablo had work to do. Nothing would stand in his way.

8 Janvier 1937

Taking a Stand

In 1937, the **Spanish Civil War** was transforming Pablo's homeland into a nightmare of bombed homes, ruined churches, and starving refugees. Hundreds of miles away, in Paris, Pablo stood in his spacious studio, dwarfed by his latest painting, *Guernica*. He had worked fervently, completing more than 60 studies before painting the giant canvas. Measuring 11 feet, 6 inches (3.5 m) tall by 25 feet, 8 inches (7.8 m) wide, the canvas dominated

OPPOSITE: A series of sketches, entitled *The Dream and Lie of Franco* (1937), served as a basis for Picasso's *Guernica*.

the studio and was too tall to stand fully upright. A ladder and long paintbrush helped Pablo reach the top half of the canvas.

After working every day for a month on the painting, Pablo felt that *Guernica* was near completion. He had invited a group of friends to his studio, and they stood around the painting, offering their opinions. But Pablo, lighting a cigarette as he stared at the canvas, remained deep in his own thoughts. He paced back and forth, walking from one end of the painting to the other.

Finally, he realized what was troubling him: the color. He had instinctively painted the scene in shades of gray, but the problem lay with the swaths of colored paper he had pinned to the canvas for the people's clothing. He had also cut one red, paper teardrop, which he moved around to the various characters in the scene. The color felt wrong to Pablo, so he began removing it, piece by piece. His friends murmured their approval, growing louder as each hint of color was stripped from the canvas. At last, Pablo tore off the bright red tear. His friends clapped and congratulated him, signaling that the painting was finished.

Inspired by the horrific bombing of the Spanish town of Guernica, the painting marked a turning point in the 55-year-old artist's life. The suffering of his fellow Spaniards and the destruction of his homeland shook Pablo from his self-centered existence. Compelled to

speak out and take action, Pablo armed himself with his paintbrush. Through his painting, he hoped to draw attention to the plight of the Spaniards and others around the world subjected to the terrors of war. While he had no intention of portraying war's realities, he said he had every intention of uncovering its truth. "Paintings," Pablo declared, "are not made to decorate apartments. They are instruments of war against brutality and darkness."

Stark and gray, *Guernica* resembles newspaper photographs of war. From a tangle of wreckage and disjointed images, the faces and bodies of the living appear in their moments of desperation. The jagged rays of the sun and one small candle scatter uneven light over the devastation, and the unimaginable is bared for all the world to see. A mother wails, holding the limp body of her dead child. A body lays trampled and dismembered. A figure calls from inside a house licked by flames. Ghostlike faces drift across the canvas. And at the center of the painting, a horse tips its head back, releasing a sharp-tongued scream.

pon *Guernica*'s completion, Pablo did not place his signature or a date on the painting. He knew that war could never be "finished" as a painting could be finished, and he felt that *Guernica* did not belong to him, but to all people who suffered the atrocities of war.

Guernica became Pablo's best-known painting, hailed as the masterpiece of his career and one of the

most powerful pieces of art created in the 20th century. But its brilliance was not immediately recognized. In 1937, at its first showing in Paris, *Guernica* received little attention from critics or the public. However, in the years that followed, especially during the brutality of **World War II**, the painting gained recognition as it traveled for exhibitions around the globe.

Pablo had painted *Guernica* as a gift to Spain, but he would not allow the painting to enter the country while the **fascist** government of Francisco Franco was in power. It was not until 1981, on the centennial of Pablo's birth, that *Guernica* was hung in Madrid's national modern art museum, Reina Sofia. It continues to hang there to this day, attracting admirers of the artist's work and those who are called to the painting's enduring truth.

"How had he captured the secret of the future? Picasso's canvas has all the horrors of the future, raising to infinity the atomic cataclysm, the world reduced to rubble, the triumph of hatred, despair, the absurd, nothingness."

— Russian journalist and novelist Ilya Ehrenburg, on *Guernica*

A Race against Time

After the bombing of Guernica, life worsened for Pablo's fellow Spaniards, as well as for Europeans across the continent. In 1939, when Pablo was 57, World War II broke out. Like all other Parisians, he faced shortages of food and fuel for the winter. However, what concerned him most was his shortage of art supplies. But his creativity didn't allow him to despair for long. Looking through the trash, Pablo began making art from "found" objects, such

OPPOSITE: Picasso developed a keen interest in pottery in his 60s; he is here shown painting an urn.

47

as sculpting a bull's head from a discarded bicycle seat
and handle bars.

n 1943, toward the end of the war, Pablo fell in love
with a young art student named Françoise Gilot.
They moved to Antibes, along the southern coast
of France, and had two children together, Claude and
Paloma. During their time in Antibes, Pablo devoted most
of his energies to ceramics and sculpture, working nearby
in the renowned ceramics town of Vallauris. His ceramics
and sculpture revealed Pablo's often whimsical nature
and his versatility as an artist. A series of his ceramic pots

Picasso and Françoise Gilot on the artist's 70th birthday, in 1951.

had female heads, and he favored eye-catching designs and bright colors in most of his creations. His sculptures ranged from large, angular structures welded from metal to clay figures of people and animals. Although he was in his late 60s, he had not stopped challenging himself to work in new directions.

Unfortunately, after 10 years together, Pablo's relationship with Françoise deteriorated. In 1953, she left him, taking the children with her to Paris. To shake the memories of his departed family, Pablo moved to La Californie, a grand house in the coastal town of Cannes. His home, cluttered with paintings, sculptures, ceramics, and many of his found treasures, rejuvenated his spirits and his work. The artist devoted himself to re-creations of many famous paintings, done in his original style.

Shortly afterward, Pablo met a beautiful French woman named Jacqueline Roque. A bit older than his usual loves, Jacqueline seemed a perfect match for the aging artist. She became more than Pablo's model and inspiration. Jacqueline became his manager, cataloging his work, arranging exhibitions, and taking care of the financial aspects of his art. In 1961, when Pablo was 79 years old, they married and moved to a smaller home in the town of Mougins, also near Cannes.

Pablo relished the seclusion he found in Mougins. Satisfied with the artistic recognition and commercial success that had graced his past, Pablo felt free to work on whatever fascinated him at the moment. Often clad in a charming combination of mismatched clothes, and sometimes working in only his bathrobe or undergar-

ments, the artist remained sprightly and vivacious well into his 80s.

Pablo received many accolades in the last decade of his life. Among them, the Picasso Museum, a museum devoted exclusively to his work, opened in Barcelona. Also, on Pablo's 90th birthday, the president of France unveiled eight of his paintings for an exhibit in the Grand Gallery of the Louvre. Pablo knew that he had earned the right to settle down, retire, and simply enjoy his last years. After all, he was a millionaire, a status rarely achieved by artists.

But, despite his sense of financial security, he still felt driven to work. There was so much more that he wished to say.

Feeling as though he were in a race against death, many of Pablo's final pictures reveal his fear of leaving the physical world. Even though his mind remained sharp, his body was gradually failing. No longer could he work into the night. He seemed smaller, as though he were shrinking, and the characteristic spark in his eyes was fading.

Finally, at the age of 91, Pablo took to his bed in Mougins, drained of most of his life. The artist had once described his endless passion by saying, "I paint just as I breathe." Even though his body was tired and his breathing shallow, Pablo continued to create. Crayons and a sheath of paper rested on a table beside his bed. And to the very end of his life, his hand glided over the paper, shaping his last breath into bold, brilliant color.

In His Words

Although Pablo Picasso wrote poetry on occasion, he never personally wrote anything about his views or opinions on art. He did, however, grant several interviews for publication. The following excerpts are from two of those interviews— the first from 1923, and the second from 1935—and provide insight into his approach to painting, the invention of Cubism, and the understanding of art.

OPPOSITE: Picasso lived a quiet and reclusive life after moving to Mougins, France, rarely venturing far from his studio.

An Interview

The following statement was made in Spanish to Marius
de Zayas. Picasso approved de Zayas's manuscript before
it was translated into English and published in The Arts,
New York, May, 1923, *under the title* Picasso Speaks.
At the time he made the statement, Picasso was painting
in the manner generally known as his "classic period."

Do Not Seek—Find!
Paris, 1923

In my opinion, to search means nothing in painting. To
find is the thing. Nobody is interested in following a man
who, with his eyes fixed on the ground, spends his life look-
ing for the pocketbook that fortune should put in his path.

    Among the several sins that I have been accused of
committing, none is more false than the one that I have, as

"He can do anything, he knows everything, succeeds at all he undertakes. . . . Child prodigy he was; prodigy he is in maturity; and prodigy of old age to come, I have no doubt."

— Writer Jacques-Émile Blanche

A portrait of José Ruiz Blasco by Picasso at age 18.

Picasso
1906

the principal objective in my work, the spirit of research. When I paint, my object is to show what I have found and not what I am looking for. In art, intentions are not sufficient and, as we say in Spanish, love must be proved by facts and not by reasons....

The idea of research has often made painting go astray, and made the artist lose himself in mental lucubrations. Perhaps this has been the principal fault of modern art. The spirit of research has poisoned those who have not fully understood all the positive and conclusive elements in modern art and has made them attempt to paint the invisible and, therefore, the unpaintable.

They speak of naturalism in opposition to modern painting. I would like to know if anyone has ever seen a natural work of art. Nature and art, being two different things, cannot be the same thing. Through art, we express *our conception of what nature is not.*

Velázquez left us his idea of the people of his epoch. Undoubtedly, they were different from what he painted them, but we cannot conceive a Philip IV in any other way than the one Velázquez painted....

And from the point of view of art, there are no concrete or abstract forms, but only forms which are more or less convincing lies. That those lies are necessary to our mental selves is beyond any doubt, as it is through them that we form our aesthetic point of view of life.

Cubism is no different from any other school of painting. The same principles and the same elements are common to all. The fact that for a long time Cubism has not been understood and that even today there are people who cannot see anything in it, means nothing. I do not read English; an English book is a blank book to me. This does not mean that the English language does not exist, and why should I blame anybody else but myself if I cannot understand what I know nothing about?

Art Does Not Evolve

I also often hear the word "evolution." Repeatedly, I am asked to explain how my painting evolved. To me, there is no past or future in art. If a work of art cannot live always in the present, it must not be considered at all. The art of the Greeks, of the Egyptians, of the great painters who lived in other times, is not an art of the past; perhaps it is more alive today than it ever was. Art does not evolve by itself; the ideas of people change and with them their mode of expression. When I hear people speak of the evolution of an artist, it seems to me that they are considering him standing between two mirrors that face each other and

Picasso with a painting that illustrates the pioneering style that radically and forever altered our concept of art.

reproduce his image an infinite number of times, and that they contemplate the successive images of one mirror as his past, and the images of the other mirror as his future, while his real image is taken as his present. They do not consider that they all are the same images in different planes....

The several manners I have used in my art must not be considered as an evolution, or as steps towards an unknown ideal of painting.... When I have found something to express, I have done it without thinking of the past or of the future. I do not believe I have used radically different elements in the different manners I have used in painting. If the subjects I have wanted to express have suggested different ways of expression, I have never hesitated to adopt them. I have never made trials nor experiments. Whenever I had something to say, I have said it in the manner in which I have felt it ought *to be said. Different motives inevitably require different methods of expression....*

Cubism

Many think that Cubism is an art of transition, an experiment which is to bring ulterior results. Those who think that way have not understood it. Cubism is not either a seed or a fetus, but an art dealing primarily with forms, and when a form is realized it is there to live its own life.... If Cubism is an art of transition I am sure that the only thing that will come out of it is another form of Cubism.

Mathematics, trigonometry, chemistry, psychoanalysis, music, and whatnot have been related to Cubism to give it an easier interpretation. All this has been pure literature, not to say nonsense, which brought bad results, blinding people with theories. Cubism has kept itself within the limits and limitations of painting, never pretending to go beyond it.

A Conversation

Christian Zervos (editor of Cahiers d'Art) *put down these remarks of Picasso immediately after a conversation with him at Boisgeloup, his country place, in 1935. When Zervos wanted to show Picasso his notes, Picasso replied: "You don't need to show them to me. The essential thing in our period of weak morale is to create enthusiasm. How many people have actually read Homer? All the same, the whole world talks of him. In this way the Homeric legend is created. A legend in this sense provokes a valuable stimulus. Enthusiasm is what we need most, we and the younger generation."*

Zervos reports, however, that Picasso did actually go over the notes and approved them informally.

Boisgeloup, 1935

It is my misfortune—and probably my delight—to use things as my passions tell me. What a miserable fate for a painter who adores blondes to have to stop himself putting them into a picture because they don't go with the basket of fruit! How awful for a painter who loathes apples to have to use them all the time because they go so well with the cloth. I put all the things I like into my pictures. The things—so much the worse for them; they just have to put up with it.

A Picture Is a Sum of Destructions

In the old days, pictures went forward towards completion by stages. Every day brought something new. A picture used to be a sum of additions. In my case, a picture is a sum of destructions. I do a picture—then I destroy it. In the end, though, nothing is lost: the red I took away from one place turns up somewhere else.

It would be very interesting to preserve photographically, not the stages, but the metamorphoses of a picture. Possibly one might then discover the path followed by the brain in materializing a dream. But there is one very odd thing—to notice that basically a picture doesn't change, that the first "vision" remains almost intact, in spite of appearances. I often ponder on a light and a dark when I have put them into a picture; I try hard to break them up by interpolating a color that will create a different effect. When the work is photographed, I note that what I put in to correct my first vision has disappeared, and that, after all, the photographic image corresponds with my first vision before the transformation I insisted on....

PABLO PICASSO

"He rarely made sketches with a future work in view;
each picture was an end, a universe in itself. He gave his
creative urge free rein, and lived only in the present."

— Daniel-Henry Kahnweiler, *Picasso's art dealer*

There Is No Abstract Art

There is no abstract art. You must always start with something. Afterwards, you can remove all traces of reality. There's no danger then, anyway, because the idea of the object will have left an indelible mark. It is what started the artist off, excited his ideas, and stirred up his emotions. Ideas and emotions will in the end be prisoners in his work....

In my Dinard pictures and my Pourville pictures, I expressed very much the same vision. However, you yourself have noticed how different the atmosphere of those painted in Brittany is from those painted in Normandy, because you recognized the light of the Dieppe cliffs. I didn't copy this light, nor did I pay it any special attention. I was simply soaked in it. My eyes saw it and my subconscious registered what they saw: my hand fixed the impression. One cannot go against nature....

Nor is there any "figurative" and "non-figurative" art. Everything appears to us in the guise of a "figure." Even in metaphysics ideas are expressed by means of symbolic "figures." See how ridiculous it is, then, to think of painting without "figuration."

The Painter Unloads His Feelings

When we invented Cubism, we had no intention whatever of inventing Cubism. We wanted simply to express what was in us. Not one of us drew up a plan of campaign, and our friends, the poets, followed our efforts attentively, but they never dictated to us. Young painters today often draw up a program to follow, and apply themselves like diligent students to performing their tasks.

The painter goes through states of fullness and evacuation. That is the whole secret of art. I go for a walk in the forest of Fontainebleau. I get "green" indigestion. I must get rid of this sensation into a picture. Green rules it. A painter paints to unload himself of feelings and visions. People seize on painting to cover up their nakedness. They get what they can wherever they can. In the end I don't believe they get anything at all. They've simply cut a coat to the measure of their own ignorance. They make everything, from God to a picture, in their own image. That is why the picture-hook is the ruination of a painting—a painting which has always had a certain significance, at least as much as the man who did it. As soon as it is bought and hung on a wall, it takes on quite a different kind of significance, and the painting is done for.

PABLO PICASSO

Timeline

1881   Pablo Ruiz Picasso is born in Málaga, Spain, on October 25.

1895   Picasso's family moves to Barcelona; Picasso enrolls at the art school La Lonja and attends for the next two years.

1896   Picasso enters his first competitions, earning exhibition in a Barcelona city show and winning an honorable mention at a show in Madrid.

1897   Picasso studies in Madrid.

1900   Picasso begins working on his own full-time and joins a circle of artists at The Four Cats in Barcelona.

1901   Picasso's Blue Period begins. He uses his mother's name, "Picasso," as his artist name.

1904   Picasso moves to Paris permanently and enters his Rose Period.

1907   Picasso shows his first Cubist painting, *Les Demoiselles d'Avignon*, to a group of friends.

1913   Picasso's Cubist paintings draw the highest bidders at auction. He becomes instantly wealthy and well known.

1918   Picasso marries Russian ballerina Olga Koklova. They have one child together.

1927   Picasso meets Marie-Thérèse Walter. She becomes his mistress, and they have a child seven years later.

1937   Picasso finishes *Guernica*. After its first exhibition in Paris, it begins traveling around the world.

1943 Picasso meets Françoise Gilot, a young art student. They live together in common-law marriage and have two children.

1953 Gilot leaves Picasso, taking the children with her to Paris.

1961 Picasso marries a French woman named Jacqueline Roque.

1963 The Picasso Museum is dedicated in Barcelona.

1971 On Picasso's 90th birthday, the Louvre exhibits eight of his paintings.

1973 Picasso dies in his sleep in Mougins, France, at the age of 91.

Selected Bibliography

Gilot, Françoise, with Carlton Lake. *Life with Picasso*. New York: Anchor / Doubleday, 1989.

O'Brian, Patrick. *Picasso: A Biography*. New York: Putnam, 1976.

Richardson, John. *A Life of Picasso: 1881–1906*. New York: Random House, 1991.

———. *A Life of Picasso: 1907–1917; the Painter of Modern Life*. New York: Random House, 1996.

Rose, Bernice B., and Bernard Ruiz Picasso, eds. *Picasso: 200 Masterworks from 1898 to 1972*. Boston: Little, Brown, 2002.

Glossary

Blue Period   Picasso's earliest period of paintings (1901–04), characterized by his use of the color blue to emphasize loneliness and isolation in his human subjects

bohemian   a word used to describe unconventional people, such as artists and writers, who typically don't follow social rules or customs

Cubism   an art movement in the early 1900s characterized by a distorted portrayal of its subjects, often showing the shapes that comprise an object and representing multiple perspectives at once

fascist   a person or group believing in fascism, a political system consisting of dictatorship, brutal suppression of any opposition, extreme nationalism, and, often, racism; Spain's Francisco Franco, Italy's Benito Mussolini, and Germany's Adolf Hitler were all fascist leaders

gypsy   the common name for the Romany people, a group of nomadic people in Europe who typically live outside of society

Louvre   France's national museum and art gallery, located in the former royal palace in Paris

Modernist   of an artistic movement in the early 1900s
                     concerned with breaking from traditional
                     forms in art and literature and finding new
                     methods of expression for the future

pre-Iberian art referring to the ancient art of the
                     inhabitants of the Iberian Peninsula, the
                     area that is now Portugal and Spain

Rose Period   Picasso's second early phase of paintings
                     (1904–06), following the Blue Period; his
                     Rose Period paintings used rose hues and
                     often focused on circus characters

Spanish Civil War the war, from 1936 to 1939, between
                     fascist powers and the established Spanish
                     republican government that ended with
                     General Francisco Franco's dictatorial
                     government winning control of the country

World War I   the war fought in Europe from 1914 to 1918
                     between the Allied Powers (France, Russia,
                     Great Britain, Italy, and the U.S.) and the
                     Central Powers (Austria-Hungary, Germany,
                     Bulgaria, and the Ottoman Empire)

World War II   a worldwide conflict that involved more
                     than 70 nations; the war was instigated by
                     German dictator Adolf Hitler in 1939 and
                     ended in 1945 with the defeat of Germany,
                     Italy, and Japan

A bronze bust of Fernande Olivier made by Picasso.

Index